Holiday ★ Histories

D0339427

Presidents' Day

Mir Tamim Ansary

WALLA WALLA
RURAL LIBRARY DISTRICT
TOUCHET

Heinemann Library
Chicago, Illinois

© 1999 Reed Educational & Professional Publishing
Published by Heinemann Library,
an imprint of Reed Educational & Professional Publishing,
Chicago, IL

Customer Service 888-454-2279

Visit our website at www.heinemannlibrary.com

All rights reserved. No part of this publication may be reproduced or transmitted in any form
or by any means, electronic or mechanical, including photocopying, recording, taping, or any
information storage and retrieval system, without permission in writing from the publisher.

Printed and bound in Hong Kong

05 04 03 02 01
10 9 8 7 6 5 4 3 2 1

Library of Congress Cataloging-in-Publication Data
Ansary, Mir Tamim, 1954-
    Presidents' Day / Mir Tamim Ansary.
        p.   cm. — (Holiday histories)
    Includes bibliographical references and index.
    Summary: Introduces Presidents' Day, explaining the historical
events behind it, how it became a holiday, and how it is observed.
    ISBN 1-57572-875-3 (lib. bdg.)   ISBN 1-58810-434-6 (pbk. bdg.)
    1. Presidents' Day—Juvenile literature. 2. Presidents—United
States—History—Juvenile literature. [1. Presidents' Day.
2. Presidents. 3. Holidays.] I. Title. II. Series: Ansary, Mir
Tamim. Holiday histories.
E176.8.A45 1998
394.261—dc21   98-14380
                                                                        CIP
                                                                        AC

Acknowledgments
The publisher would like to thank the following for permission to reprduce photographs:

Cover: AP/Wide World

The Picture Cube, Inc./Kindra Clineff, p. 4; Photo Researchers/Joe Sohm, p. 6; Corbis-Bettmann, p.
7; The Granger Collection, pp. 8, 10, 11, 12, 14, 20, 22, 23, 25(top), 26; Super Stock, pp. 9, 15, 18,
21, 27; Archive/Photo Researchers, p. 13; Bettmann Archive, p. 16; AP/Wide World, p. 24;
Reuters/Corbis-Bettmann, p. 28(left); UPI/Corbis-Bettmann, p. 28(right).

Every effort has been made to contact copyright holders of any material reproduced in this book.
Any omissions will be rectified in subsequent printings if notice is given to the publisher.

Some words are shown in bold, **like this**. You can find
out what they mean by looking in the glossary.

Contents

WALLA WALLA
RURAL LIBRARY DISTRICT
TOUCHET

A Winter Holiday

It is the middle of February. Christmas vacation ended long ago. Summer is still far away. Thank goodness for Presidents' Day!

★

This holiday is on the third Monday in February. What a good time for a day off.

★

Honoring Our Leader

On Presidents' Day, we **honor** our country's leader. This person is chosen by the people. Every four years, grown-ups vote for a new president.

The president's house, The White House, in Washington, D.C.

Sometimes they **elect** the same leader again. But no one may be president more than twice. After that, someone else gets a turn.

Ronald Reagan, at left, became the fortieth president in 1981.

How Presidents' Day Began

When your grandparents were born, Presidents' Day was not celebrated. In its place were two other holidays. Every state celebrated George Washington's Birthday on February 22.

Many states celebrated Abraham Lincoln's Birthday, too. That falls on February 12. Washington was our first president and Lincoln was our sixteenth.

The Thirteen Colonies

Before Washington's time, the United States was not a country. It was a group of thirteen little **colonies**. The **colonists** had come from Europe.

The leader of these colonies was the king of England. The colonists had to pay the king money. They had to obey his rules and his soldiers.

The American Revolution

The **colonists** got tired of this. They told the king they were a new country. The king did not agree. The Revolutionary War broke out.

George Washington led the American
armies. And they won. The colonists were
free to set up a new country. But what kind?

★

A New Democracy

Back then, most countries had kings. Kings had total power. When they died, their sons almost always took over.

But the Americans decided to try something
new. They set up a democracy. In a
democracy, the people have the power.
They choose their own leaders.

★

Our First President

The people of the United States chose George Washington as their first leader. In fact, they **elected** him twice. After that, some people even asked him to be king.

But Washington did something few have done. He said no to power. He did not want to be president for a third time. This may have been one of his greatest deeds.

The Country Splits

Abraham Lincoln was **elected** president in 1860. This was a **tense** time. Some people in our country had **slaves**. Others wanted to end **slavery**.

The Southern states tried to split away from the United States. Lincoln would not let them. He went to war to stop the **rebels**. The Civil War began.

★

Why We Honor Lincoln

The Civil War raged until 1865. It ended **slavery** in the United States. It gave this country a new start as a land of freedom.

★

We **honor** Lincoln for keeping the United States together. We honor him for helping to end slavery. Many Americans think he is our greatest president.

Jefferson and Wilson

But there have been other great presidents. There was Thomas Jefferson. He was our third president. He helped to **found** our country.

There was Woodrow Wilson, our twenty-eighth president. He led the United States through World War One.

Franklin D. Roosevelt

In 1930, much of the world became very poor. Many people lost their jobs. People stood in line for food. This time was called the Great **Depression**.

Our thirty-second president helped end this depression. Then he led our country through World War Two. His name was Franklin D. Roosevelt.

Our Right to Choose Greatness

Our country **elected** 43 presidents in its first 211 years. Not all of them were perfect. Some are hardly even remembered.

Warren G. Harding,
twenty-ninth president

Millard Fillmore,
thirteenth president

William Henry Harrison,
ninth president

Presidents Washington, Jefferson, Theodore Roosevelt, and Lincoln on Mount Rushmore National Memorial in South Dakota

But some of our presidents were truly great. And they rose to power when they were needed most. Was this just luck? Probably not.

★

Celebrating Our Democracy

We the people chose the great presidents. We **elected** the leaders we needed in times of trouble. You may say we celebrate ourselves on Presidents' Day.

We celebrate the fact that we have a president and not a king. We celebrate our democracy. That is why, on this day, we now **honor** all our presidents.

Important Dates

Presidents' Day

1607	First English colony is founded in North America
1775	The American Revolution begins
1776	American colonists declare their independence
1781	Americans win their independence
1789–1796	George Washington is president of the United States
1801–1809	Thomas Jefferson is president
1860–1865	Abraham Lincoln is president
1913–1921	Woodrow Wilson is president
1929	The Great Depression begins
1933–1945	Franklin D. Roosevelt is president
1968	Presidents' Day replaces Washington's and Lincoln's birthdays

WALLA WALLA
RURAL LIBRARY DISTRICT
TOUCHET

Glossary

colonies group of people who live far from home but follow the laws of their homeland

colonists people of a colony

depression time when most people are out of work and poor

elect to choose a leader

found to start something new

honor to show respect for someone

rebels people who fight against their own government

slaves people who are owned by and work for other people

slavery to use people as slaves

tense full of worry

More Books to Read

Alden, Laura. *Presidents' Day*. Danbury, Conn: Children's Press, 1994.

Penner, Lucille. *The Story of American Holidays*. New York: Simon & Schuster Children's, 1993.

Sorensen, Lynda. *Presidents' Day*. Vero Beach, Fla: Rourke Press, 1994.

Index

WALLA WALLA
RURAL LIBRARY DISTRICT
TOUCHET